I0805126

STUDY GUIDE

Justified by Faith Alone

R.C. Sproul

LIGONIER MINISTRIES
Renew your Mind.
LIGONIER.ORG | 800-435-4343

421 Ligonier Court, Sanford, FL 32771
E-mail: info@ligonier.org

Printed in the United States of America.

1

A Doctrine for Today

INTRODUCTION

The doctrine of justification by faith alone is essential to our understanding of the gospel itself. In this introductory lesson, Dr. Sproul argues that justification by faith alone remains, to this day, a doctrine with eternal consequences.

LESSON OBJECTIVE

To demonstrate how the doctrine of justification by faith alone is as important today as it was at the time of the Reformation

SCRIPTURE READING

The Lord is slow to anger and abounding in steadfast love, forgiving iniquity and transgression, but he will by no means clear the guilty.

—Numbers 14:18

LECTURE OUTLINE

A. The Protestant Reformation was the deepest fracture in the entire history of the church, which shows the importance of the doctrine of justification by faith alone.
   1. One church historian has noted that the Reformation is over.
      a. The battle in the sixteenth century was a vicious battle, yet it has cooled off to the point that it is wrongly suggested that any debate over the doctrine of justification is no longer needed.
   2. The split within the church often led to violence.
      a. A monarch in England was nicknamed "Bloody Mary."
         i. She tried to restore Catholicism to England through radical persecution.
         ii. People were tortured and killed over an issue that has eternal consequences—justification by faith alone.

3. The church has always had to deal with division and debates over theology.
    a. In the fourth century, Arius denied the deity of Christ, which led to the Council of Nicea and the Nicene Creed.
    b. In the fifth century, the church battled Eutyches and Nestorius by forming the Council of Chalcedon to further define the person of Christ.
    c. Yet all of these controversies pale in comparison to the split that occurred during the Protestant Reformation.

B. Luther was willing to let the church be torn over the issue of justification.
1. Luther would allow this for the sake of those who were not hearing the gospel.
2. The Latin phrase *post tenebras lux* means "after darkness light."
    a. Luther believed that the gospel had fallen into darkness.
        i. The Middle Ages were a period of unprecedented church corruption.
        ii. The gospel was hidden under the machinations of the liturgies of the church.
3. Luther understood the Reformation as the recapturing and recovering of nothing less than the gospel itself.
    a. Rome believed that allowing people to read the Bible apart from the interpretation of the church would "open a floodgate of iniquity" that would result in countless churches' claiming to be the true church.
    b. Luther was aware that this could happen, but he believed that keeping the gospel away from the people was inexcusable.
4. Luther believed that the doctrine of justification by faith was the article upon which the church stands or falls.
    a. He believed that without the doctrine of justification by faith, Christianity would be lost.
    b. Without the gospel, the church would have no reason to exist.

C. The doctrine of justification by faith alone answers the question, "What must I do to be saved?"
1. The biggest problem we face is that God is holy, and we are not.
    a. How can we be made right with Him?
    b. God cannot simply redeem people apart from the process of justification without negotiating His righteousness.
    c. God can maintain His own righteousness and redeem unjust people through Jesus Christ (Rom. 3:26).
2. Justification by faith is not an irrelevant doctrine because it centers on the question of how a person is saved.
    a. Calvin stated that justification is the hinge on which everything turns.
        i. Calvin may have in mind the many times Christ used the metaphor of the door to speak of salvation (John 10:9).
        ii. Calvin understood the phrase "justification by faith alone" to be simple shorthand for "justification by Christ alone."

b. Many people may consider metaphors like the ones above to be exaggerating the importance of justification by faith alone and discounting the Reformation to a mere misunderstanding.
    i. They ignore all the failed attempts that were made in the sixteenth century to heal the rift over justification.
    ii. These attempts failed because the differences over justification were not imagined—they were real and remain to this day.

D. Believing specifically in the doctrine of justification by faith alone does not save us.
1. The critique that we are not saved by believing a particular doctrine has been recently leveled against those who hold to Reformed theology.
    a. The doctrine of justification by faith alone actually refutes the idea that you can be saved by believing the doctrine of justification by faith alone.
2. It is not the doctrine that saves; it is Christ who saves.
    a. Justification is putting our trust in Christ alone.
3. Simply affirming the doctrine of justification by faith alone saves no one, but what happens if you deny the doctrine of justification by faith alone?
    a. If you deny the doctrine of justification by faith alone, then you are denying that Christ alone saves you.
4. Both Roman Catholics and Protestants believe that the proper understanding of the doctrine of salvation is crucial for our everlasting redemption.
    a. The doctrine of justification by faith alone is not a minor issue and is critical to the church's understanding of the gospel itself.

STUDY QUESTIONS

1. The famous statement that "the doctrine of justification by faith alone is the article upon which the church stands or falls" was originally made by ________.
    a. R.C. Sproul
    b. Martin Luther
    c. John Calvin
    d. John Knox

2. Dr. Sproul mentions the ________ century as hosting some major controversies in church history.
    a. Fourth
    b. Fifth
    c. Sixteenth
    d. All of the above

3. Martin Luther did not foresee the difficulties of allowing the Bible to be published in a common language.
    a. True
    b. False

4. John Calvin uses the metaphor of a ________ to describe justification.
   a. House
   b. Hinge
   c. Lock
   d. Key

5. Some scholars disregard the importance of the Reformation.
   a. True
   b. False

DISCUSSION QUESTIONS

1. Why is the doctrine of justification by faith alone as relevant today as it was at the time of the Reformation?

2. Some modern scholars state that the Reformation is over. What are they ignoring in their assertion?

3. What is the difference between putting our trust in the doctrine of justification by faith alone and putting our trust in Christ alone?

4. What is the danger of denying the doctrine of justification by faith alone?

2

Martin Luther

INTRODUCTION

Martin Luther's role in the Reformation cannot be overstated. In this lesson, Dr. Sproul explains how the life of Martin Luther is essential to the historical framework of the Reformation and its central importance for the doctrine of justification by faith alone.

LESSON OBJECTIVE

To look at the defining moments of Martin Luther's life that led up to his personal discovery of the doctrine of justification by faith alone

SCRIPTURE READING

. . . upon him was the chastisement that brought us peace . . .

—Isaiah 53:5b

LECTURE OUTLINE

A. Understanding the life of Martin Luther will help us better understand the doctrine of justification by faith alone.
   1. Luther was born in 1483 in Eisleben, Germany.
      a. The precise date of his birth is uncertain (November 20 or December 7).
   2. Though the majority of his life was spent away from Eisleben, Luther died there in 1546.
   3. Luther's father, Hans Luther, wanted Martin to become a lawyer.
      a. Luther studied law at the University of Erfurt and was an excellent student.
   4. Luther's life reveals that he tended to have a crisis about every five years.
      a. His first crisis, beginning in 1505, was while he was a student at Erfurt.

B. In 1505, Martin Luther vowed to become a monk.
   1. Luther was on his way to visit his parents from the University of Erfurt when he became caught in a violent thunderstorm.
   2. Luther cried out, "Save me, St. Anne! I will become a monk."
      a. St. Anne was the mother of Mary and was the special saint for miners and all those involved in dangerous enterprises.
   3. Luther survived the storm and when returning to the University of Erfurt gathered his belongings, said his goodbyes, and went to the Augustinian monastery in Erfurt.
      a. Luther would become a monk, to his father's consternation.
   4. Luther was ordained in Erfurt in 1507.
      a. The irony of Luther's ordination is that the bishop who condemned John Hus was buried at Erfurt a century earlier.
         i. John Hus was accused of heresy because he denied the infallibility of the church.
         ii. Before being burned at the stake, Hus declared: "a swan will come after me that you will not be able to silence."
      b. Luther's ordination consisted of laying prostrate in the shape of a cross at the base of the altar in the monastery in Erfurt.
         i. Luther was ordained on top of where the bishop who condemned John Hus was buried.
         ii. In an apocryphal telling of the story, you can imagine the bishop replying to Hus' declaration, "Over my dead body!"
      c. Luther is considered the swan anticipated by Hus.

C. Martin Luther's life as a monk was full of great anxiety and torment.
   1. Luther was an extremely productive and well-behaved monk, but he was extremely meticulous about his daily confessions.
   2. Luther was known to confess the sins he had committed over the past day for upwards to two hours.
      a. Luther would often remember a sin he forgot to confess and lose the peace he had received from absolution before he even returned to his room.
      b. Some historians have believed that Luther's behavior during this period was evident of his insanity, but Luther approached God's law with a lawyer's mind.
   3. Luther understood that he couldn't possibly love God with all his heart, soul, mind, and strength while loving his neighbor as himself.
      a. Luther understood that this was the greatest commandment, and his inability to keep it must have been the greatest transgression.
   4. Luther could not escape the guilt he was experiencing from breaking the law of God.
      a. Luther would enter into periods of self-flagellation and extreme fasting to no relief, and even his religious vocation could not console him.

D. In 1510, Martin Luther was asked to represent the Erfurt monastery on a visit to Rome.
   1. Luther was happy to be selected because he believed that one of the most significant things you could do to acquire salvation was to make a pilgrimage.
      a. The two great sites of pilgrimage were Jerusalem and Rome.
      b. The pilgrimage to Rome, the Holy City, was worth a substantial amount of indulgences.
      c. Luther could not use these indulgences himself, so he dedicated the pilgrimage to his grandparents.
   2. Luther traveled for months on foot all the way from Germany to Rome to only experience raw disillusionment.
      a. The priests in Rome were openly involved with both male and female prostitutes.
      b. The priests were reciting the Mass for a fee and would say the Mass as fast as they possibly could to increase their own personal gain.
      c. Julius II, a Borgia, was the pope at the time of Luther's pilgrimage, and he was one of the most corrupt popes in history.
   3. Luther's greatest disillusionment came during his visit to the *Scala Sacra*, the sacred stairs in the Lateran Church.
      a. The *Scala Sacra* was the staircase that Jesus walked up and down during His trial before Pontius Pilate.
      b. Crusaders dismantled the staircase and brought it to Rome.
      c. The staircase was the focal point of any pilgrimage to Rome.
         i. Reciting the "Our Father" and the "Hail Mary" on your knees on each step would gain enough indulgences to reduce a family's time in purgatory.
         ii. Even today, the *Scala Sacra* is still visited, and there is a sign advertising how many indulgences going up them is worth.
      d. Luther went up the stairs on his hands and knees, and when he got to the top, he stood up and mumbled, "Who knows if it is true?"

STUDY QUESTIONS

1. Martin Luther vowed to _________ to become a monk.
   a. Mary
   b. St. Anne
   c. St. Agatha
   d. St. Martha

2. Martin Luther belonged to the _________ monastery in Wittenberg.
   a. Benedictine
   b. Dominican
   c. Augustinian
   d. Franciscan

3. Martin Luther was ordained in _________.
    a. Wittenberg
    b. Eisleben
    c. Erfurt
    d. Rome

4. John Hus was charged with heresy because of his view of justification by faith alone.
    a. True
    b. False

5. Martin Luther devoted his pilgrimage to Rome to his _________.
    a. Monastery
    b. Grandparents
    c. Mother
    d. Father

6. The *Scala Sacra* were originally built in Rome.
    a. True
    b. False

DISCUSSION QUESTIONS

1. How does Dr. Sproul defend Martin Luther and his incessant confession of sin against the charge of insanity?

2. What does Luther's life as a monk teach us about how we should view our own sin?

3. Why were the lives of the priests in Rome so upsetting to Luther?

4. What does the *Scala Sacra* reveal about the continued importance of the Reformation?

3

The Ninety-Five Theses

INTRODUCTION

Martin Luther's discovery of the imputation of Christ's righteousness to the believer changed everything. In this lesson, Dr. Sproul explains how this discovery was a precursor to the Reformation.

LESSON OBJECTIVES

1. To communicate the significance of Martin Luther's conversion
2. To explore the history that led up to the Ninety-Five Theses

SCRIPTURE READING

For in it the righteousness of God is revealed from faith for faith.

—Romans 1:17a

LECTURE OUTLINE

A. In 1515, Martin Luther experienced the supreme crisis that was ultimately the motivation for the entire Reformation.
   1. Luther had been studying theology and biblical studies for his doctoral degree in Erfurt.
   2. In 1510, Frederick, elector of Saxony, started a new university in Wittenberg.
      a. Frederick wanted an exceptional faculty and asked Luther to lecture at the university.
      b. Luther lectured at the university for two years and went back to Erfurt.
      c. Luther returned to Wittenberg and began a series of lectures on the Psalms and, in 1515, began a series of lectures on Romans.
   3. Luther was preparing his lectures on Romans when he read an essay from Augustine on the letter and the Spirit.
      a. Augustine cited Romans 1:17: "The righteousness of God is revealed from faith for faith, as it is written, 'The righteous shall live by faith.'"

   b. Augustine wrote that the righteousness Paul was referring to is a righteousness that God provides for people who are not righteous.
4. Luther considered his realization of the imputation of the righteousness of Christ to be the moment of his conversion.
   a. Luther's conversion after all those years of guilt and torment made him able to stand against the hostility he received from what seemed to be the entire world.
   b. Luther began to see justification on virtually every page of the Bible as confirmation of his newfound understanding of Romans 1.

B. In 1517, Martin Luther tacked the Ninety-Five Theses on the castle church door at Wittenberg with respect to the sale of indulgences.
   1. The Hohenzollern dynasty wanted to have greater power and influence throughout Germany.
      a. In 1513, three bishoprics (Magdeburg, Halberstadt, and Mainz) were vacant, and Albert, a Hohenzollern prince, wanted to occupy all three.
      b. The archbishopric of Mainz was the highest ecclesiastical authority in all of Germany.
   2. The papacy at this time was very corrupt, and the only way to gain all three bishoprics was to purchase them for the pope, but the sale of church offices violated biblical and ecclesiastical prohibitions.
      a. The practice of selling church offices was called simony after the account of Simon Magus' attempting to buy the power of the Holy Spirit (Acts 8:9—24).
      b. No one could occupy more than one bishopric at the same time.
      c. Albert was only twenty-three years old—too young to be consecrated as a bishop.
   3. Albert nonetheless negotiated with the pope a price of 10,000 ducats for the archbishopric of Mainz alone and also secured the other bishoprics.
      a. The Fuggers, the largest bank in Germany, brokered the deal between Albert and the pope.
   4. An indulgence program was introduced in order to raise the money to pay for the bishoprics.
      a. Indulgences became tied to the sacrament of penance and the works of satisfaction that one could do to be restored to saving faith by extending those works of satisfaction to almsgiving.
      b. Indulgences grew from being able to reduce the time one would spend in purgatory to completely freeing one from purgatory.
      c. Alms had to be given genuinely from the heart to count as a work of satisfaction.
   5. The church expanded the indulgences program for Pope Leo X to raise money for the completion of St. Peter's Basilica, and Johann Tetzel was commissioned to bring the new indulgences program to Germany.

   a. Tetzel was an excellent salesman who utilized pomp and pageantry in announcing that indulgences would be sold weeks before he arrived in German villages with the papal bull.
   b. Tetzel used a massive holy procession where he would usher the papal bull through the town on a gold-embroidered or velvet cushion.
   c. Tetzel would say, "Every time a guilder in the kettle rings, a soul from purgatory springs."
6. Johann Tetzel sold indulgences very close to Electoral Saxony, where Wittenberg was, and many of Luther's congregation took part in the sale of indulgences from Tetzel.
   a. Out of a pastoral concern, Luther was outraged at the sale of indulgences.
7. Luther posted the Ninety-Five Theses to invite faculty members at the University of Wittenberg to discuss the issue of indulgences.
   a. Luther posted the theses in Latin, which is a sure sign that he was asking for a scholarly colloquium and not making a public declaration.
   b. Students from the university were so amazed by the Ninety-Five Theses that they translated them into German.
   c. The Ninety-Five Theses spread throughout Germany with the help of the Gutenberg printing press.
   d. Luther could have never anticipated what was to happen next.
8. Luther was eventually brought before the Diet of Worms in 1521.
   a. Luther refused to recant.

STUDY QUESTIONS

1. Luther struggled with the idea of God's _________.
   a. Wrath
   b. Justice
   c. Righteousness
   d. All of the above

2. The beginning of Luther's understanding of justification by faith developed while he was preparing lectures on the Psalms.
   a. True
   b. False

3. It was the insights of _________ that gave Martin Luther a clear understanding of "the righteousness of God."
   a. Athanasius
   b. Aquinas
   c. Augustine
   d. Anselm

4. The accounting of Christ's righteousness to the Christian is termed ________.
   a. Justification
   b. Propitiation
   c. Expiation
   d. Imputation

5. The Ninety-Five Theses were Luther's formal statement on the doctrine of justification by faith alone.
   a. True
   b. False

6. ________ authorized the sale of indulgences.
   a. Julius II
   b. Johann Tetzel
   c. Albert
   d. Leo X

DISCUSSION QUESTIONS

1. Why was Luther outraged by the sale of indulgences?

2. Why was the practice of selling church offices named simony?

3. What evidence do we have that Luther was not expecting the dawning of the Reformation in posting the Ninety-Five Theses?

4. How was Luther able to stand against the criticism of the university, the church, and virtually the world?

4

The Roman Catholic View

INTRODUCTION

The best way to understand the Reformed view of justification is in comparison to the Roman Catholic view of justification. In this lesson, Dr. Sproul reviews the Roman Catholic view of justification as defined at the Council of Trent.

LESSON OBJECTIVE

To present the Roman Catholic view of justification in order to contrast it with the Reformed doctrine of justification by faith alone

SCRIPTURE READING

He has delivered us from the domain of darkness and transferred us to the kingdom of his beloved Son, in whom we have redemption, the forgiveness of sins.

—Colossians 1:13–14

LECTURE OUTLINE

A. The best way to understand the Reformation's concept of justification is against the backdrop of the Roman Catholic view of justification.
   1. Martin Luther wrote the Ninety-Five Theses to raise questions about the system of doctrine that was associated with indulgences.
      a. The Ninety-Five Theses were not primarily addressing justification, but Luther did raise questions that connected Rome's understanding of indulgences and its view of justification.
   2. The Roman Catholic doctrine of justification took centuries to develop.
      a. Rome's system of salvation is referred to as "sacerdotalism."
      b. Sacerdotalism is the means by which salvation is wrought through the ministrations of the church and the priesthood.

3. Rome's doctrine of justification was fully defined as part of the Counter-Reformation's threefold reaction against Protestantism.
    a. The Spanish Inquisition sought to discover and torture Protestants.
    b. The Jesuits were founded by Ignatius of Loyola to address the intellectual issues of the day.
    c. An international ecumenical council, the Council of Trent, was called.

B. The sixth session of the Council of Trent dealt with the Roman Catholic view of justification.
  1. Some important points must be noted before discussing Rome's view of justification.
      a. References to the decision of Trent are sometimes called "Tridentine."
      b. The papacy still unequivocally affirms the decrees and canons of the Council of Trent.
      c. Protestants and Catholics misrepresent each other on the issue of justification (i.e., Protestants believe that faith plays no part in the Catholic system of justification).
  2. Rome teaches that the first step in justification is the sacrament of baptism.
      a. Baptism is the "instrumental cause of justification."
          i. Aristotelian distinctions of causality (material, formal, efficient, and final cause) are commonly used in discussing justification.
          ii. Baptism is the instrument by which a person is initially justified.
      b. A person is infused with the righteousness of Christ during baptism.
          i. This is called "justifying grace."
          ii. Rome uses the language of a substance (grace) being poured into the soul, which it then inhabits.
          iii. Protestants do not think of grace in substantive language but as an activity of God.
          iv. Baptism works *ex opere operato*: if you are baptized, you receive the infusion of grace and are in a state of justification.
  3. A person must next cooperate with the infused grace to stay in the state of justification.
      a. If a person cooperates with the infused grace, then he is righteous in the sight of God, because he is inherently righteous.
      b. A person remains in the state of justification until he commits a mortal sin.
  4. Rome distinguishes between venial sin and mortal sin.
      a. Venial sin is real sin that needs to be confessed and forgiven but does not destroy saving grace.
      b. Mortal sin kills the grace of justification that is infused into the soul.
      c. A person can have saving faith and still commit mortal sin, but if he commits mortal sin and dies in mortal sin, he goes to hell.

5. Rome views faith as a necessary condition for justification but not a sufficient one.
    a. Catholics believe that a person can have true faith but not be justified.
    b. Protestants believe that a person who has true faith is justified.
6. Rome teaches that faith has a threefold function with respect to justification.
    a. Faith is the initiation, the first step, of justification.
    b. Faith is the foundation upon which justification is established.
    c. Faith is the root, the core, of justification.

C. The sacrament of penance is at the core and center of the controversy in the sixteenth century.
1. The sacrament of penance answers the question, "How does one get back their justification after committing mortal sin?"
    a. Someone cannot be rebaptized because it is an indelible mark that can never be lost.
    b. Rome declared at Trent that a person needs the "second plank of justification" to recover the state of justification.
2. Confession is the first part of the sacrament of penance.
    a. A person must confess his sin to a priest.
    b. Confession must be genuine.
        i. Attrition is repentance that stems from the fear of punishment.
        ii. Contrition is repentance that stems from a broken and contrite heart (Ps. 51).
3. Priestly absolution is the second part of the sacrament of penance.
    a. The Bible teaches that we are to confess our sins to one another and that God is faithful to forgive, so confession and assurance of pardon are not bad things (James 5:16; 1 John 1:9).
    b. A priest is not exercising some inherent power to forgive sins; being consecrated a priest gives him the authority to pronounce the forgiveness of God upon a penitent person.
4. Works of satisfaction are the third part of the sacrament of penance.
    a. Works of satisfaction are where works come into play in the Roman Catholic equation of justification.
    b. Saying "Hail Mary" and "Our Father," giving alms, and doing other good works are all part of the works of satisfaction to gain justification.
    c. Works of satisfaction give a person congruous merit.
        i. Condign merit is for works that require a blessing or reward from God.
        ii. Congruous merit is for works that make it fitting for God to reward them by restoring a person to a state of justification.
5. A person can only stay in a state of justification if they do not commit mortal sin but can always return by the sacrament of penance again and again.
    a. If a person dies in mortal sin, he goes to hell.
    b. If a person dies with any impurity, he goes to purgatory.
        i. Purgatory is a place that purges a person of his impurities.

6. Ultimately, a person will not get into heaven unless he is inherently righteous.
   a. That is Rome's version of the gospel.
   b. It is in radical contrast to the Reformation's view of justification, in which if a person has faith, he has heaven.

STUDY QUESTIONS

1. The Roman view of faith is that it is necessary and sufficient for salvation.
   a. True
   b. False

2. The Roman Catholic doctrine of justification was not officially defined until ________.
   a. Lateran I
   b. Trent
   c. Vatican I
   d. Vatican II

3. Ignatius of Loyola established the ________ as part of the Counter- Reformation.
   a. Spanish Inquisition
   b. Council of Trent
   c. Society of Jesus
   d. All of the above

4. The center of the controversy during the sixteenth century was the sacrament of ________.
   a. Baptism
   b. Confirmation
   c. Eucharist
   d. Penance

5. Baptism is the ________ cause of justification in the Roman system of salvation.
   a. Instrumental
   b. Material
   c. Formal
   d. Final

6. Justification is solely by merit according to the teaching of the Roman Catholic Church.
   a. True
   b. False

DISCUSSION QUESTIONS

1. What is the significance of the reaffirmation of the Council of Trent in the Catechism of the Catholic Church in 1992?

2. How do Protestants misrepresent the Roman Catholic view of justification?

3. What do Protestants commonly misunderstand about priestly absolution?

4. How is Rome's version of the gospel in radical contrast with that of the Reformation?

5

Defining Our Terms

INTRODUCTION

Defining terms is critical to understanding and communicating the Protestant position on justification. In this lesson, Dr. Sproul concludes our study of the Roman Catholic view and begins to define the terms in the phrase *justification by faith alone*.

LESSON OBJECTIVES

1. To conclude the basic overview of the Roman Catholic understanding of justification
2. To define the terms *justification* and *by* in the phrase *justification by faith alone*
3. To contrast the Roman Catholic and Protestant views of justification

SCRIPTURE READING

. . . to an inheritance that is imperishable, undefiled, and unfading, kept in heaven for you, who by God's power are being guarded through faith . . .

—1 Peter 1:4–5

LECTURE OUTLINE

A. We must look at the treasury of merit to conclude our overview of the Roman Catholic system of justification.
   1. The treasury of merit is critical to the whole concept of indulgences.
      a. When Luther posted the Ninety-Five Theses, he still essentially believed the Roman system, but the treasury of merit was one of the areas that made him begin to question it seriously.
   2. The concept of indulgences developed gradually over the history of the Roman Catholic Church.
      a. It is ultimately based on the authority Christ gave to Peter in giving him the keys of the kingdom (Matt. 16:19).
      b. This entailed the authority to dispense indulgences.

3. The treasury of merit exists to provide merit for those who do not have enough merit of their own.
   a. Christ is the chief depositor to the treasury of merit, but the concept of the treasury of merit still exists in the Roman communion.
   b. The merits of Mary and the merits of the saints are added to the treasury of merit.
4. The treasury of merit exists so that people can get into heaven.
   a. Very few people die and go directly to heaven, according to the Roman Catholic view.
   b. The majority of people who die go to purgatory to have their impurities purged.
      i. Purgatory is not hell; it is not a place of punishment.
      ii. People in purgatory do not have sufficient merit to get them directly into heaven.
   c. The few who go directly to heaven have sufficient merit as well as supererogatory merit.
      i. Works that go beyond the call of duty produce supererogatory merit.
      ii. Supererogatory merit is more than is required to get into heaven, allowing for the excess to be deposited into the treasury of merit.
   d. When indulgences are purchased, withdrawals are made from the treasury of merit for those in purgatory.
5. The Roman Catholic view of justification is in direct contrast to justification by faith alone.

B. We begin introducing the Protestant view of justification by defining the terms in the phrase "justification by faith alone."
   1. "Justification" comes from the Latin *iustificare*—meaning "to make just" or "to make righteous."
   2. The Latin fathers developed the doctrine of justification from their study of the Latin Vulgate.
      a. The Latin *iustificare* is drawn from the legal structure of the Roman system of law.
      b. "To make righteous" means that a person who is not righteous is made righteous in and of themselves.
         i. From the Reformed perspective, the process of being made truly righteous is called sanctification.
         ii. We believe that justification is followed by sanctification.
      c. Sanctification precedes justification in the Roman view because God would not pronounce someone just if he had not yet truly become just.
   3. The Greek word *dikaioō* means "to count" or "to reckon" as righteous.
      a. *Dikaioō* leads to the Reformed view that while we are still unrighteous, God declares us righteous by applying to us the righteousness of Christ through imputation.

4. Luther's motto *simul justus et peccator* defines the state of affairs whereby God counts us as righteous even though we are not righteous in and of ourselves.
   a. *Simul justus et peccator* means "at the same time just and sinner."
   b. This does not violate the law of noncontradiction, which states that something cannot be "A" and "not-A" at the same time and in the same relationship.
   c. In and of ourselves we remain sinners, but we are righteous by virtue of Christ's righteousness.
5. Imputation has always been the one thing that has caused the many attempts to resolve the theological conflict of the Reformation to fail.
   a. Rome has always rejected the idea that we are justified on the basis of an imputed righteousness.
   b. Luther referred to imputed righteousness as *alenum iustitiam*, an "alien righteousness," a righteousness that is *extra nos*, "outside of us."

C. The second word in the phrase "justification by faith alone" that needs to be defined is the word *by*.
1. *By* is a simple term that has to do with the means by which something occurs.
   a. Remember that the instrumental means of justification is baptism in the Roman Catholic view.
   b. It is important to look at the philosophical language used to describe motion and change to understand a phrase like *instrumental means*.
2. Aristotle developed a system of classification to describe the way things change using the illustration of a sculpture.
   a. The efficient cause, the main cause of change, would be the sculptor.
   b. The material cause, the matter out of which something is changed, would be the slab of marble.
      i. Note that there is no material cause for creation, so God is both the efficient and sufficient cause because he created the world *ex nihilo*.
   c. The formal cause, the form something is changed into, would be the idea or blueprint the sculptor has in mind to create the sculpture.
   d. The final cause, the reason something is changed, would be the purpose for the sculpture.
   e. The instrumental cause, the things used to bring the change about, would be the hammer and the chisel.
      i. Rome believes that baptism is the instrumental cause by which a person is infused by grace and justified.
      ii. Protestants believe that faith is the instrumental cause of justification.
3. Both Catholics and Protestants have expanded on Aristotle's categories by adding another specific cause called the "meritorious cause."
   a. The Roman view would be that the meritorious cause for God to declare a person righteous is because that person is righteous.
   b. The Reformed view would be that the meritorious cause for God to declare a person righteous is because Christ is righteous.

4. The phrase *justification by faith alone* is simply shorthand for *justification by Christ alone*.
    a. Justification is by grace alone, through faith alone, and in Christ alone.

STUDY QUESTIONS

1. Purgatory is a place of punishment.
    a. True
    b. False

2. People who go to purgatory do not have ________ merit to get them into heaven.
    a. Necessary
    b. Sufficient
    c. Condign
    d. Christ's

3. ________ merit is deposited into the treasury of merit.
    a. Condign
    b. Congruent
    c. Supererogatory
    d. All of the above

4. The chief deposit to the treasury of merit is the sum total of all of the saint's merit.
    a. True
    b. False

5. *Dikaioō* means "to ________ righteous."
    a. Make
    b. Declare
    c. Become
    d. None of the above

6. The word *by* in the phrase *justification by faith alone* is most closely related to ________ cause.
    a. Final
    b. Formal
    c. Material
    d. Instrumental

DISCUSSION QUESTIONS

1. What are the implications of the treasury of merit's containing not only Christ's merit but also the merit of Mary and the saints?

2. How is the Roman view of justification like the Protestant view of sanctification? How is it different?

3. How does the Latin term for justification differ from the Greek term for justification?

4. How is Luther's motto *simul justus et peccator* not a violation of the law of noncontradiction?

6

By Faith Alone

INTRODUCTION

What are the essential elements of saving faith, and where should it be placed? In this lesson, Dr. Sproul continues to define the terms in the phrase *justification by faith alone* by taking a closer look at a saving faith that is in Christ alone.

LESSON OBJECTIVES

1. To define the terms *faith* and *alone* in the phrase *justification by faith alone*
2. To highlight distinctions within saving faith
3. To underline the importance of imputation

SCRIPTURE READING

For by grace you have been saved through faith. And this is not your own doing; it is the gift of God.

—Ephesians 2:8

LECTURE OUTLINE

A. What does the word *faith* mean in the formula of *justification by faith alone*?
   1. Roman Catholics believed Luther was teaching licentious libertinism or antinomianism.
      a. Luther was not teaching that people could live however they wanted on the basis of works' not being required for justification.
      b. Luther had the task of defining what saving faith truly meant.
   2. Historically, scholars have differed as to how the Reformers expanded an understanding of the elements of saving faith.
      a. Francis Turretin included as many as eight subtle, nuanced elements of saving faith.

b. Gordon Clark believed that there are only two components of saving faith.
c. The customary Reformed understanding of saving faith is that there are three distinct elements.

B. The three distinct elements of saving faith are *notitia, assensus*, and *fiducia*.

1. *Notitia* is the information one has to believe to be justified.
   a. We need the basic information about Christ to be justified.
   b. *Notitia* consists of the essentials of the gospel.
2. *Assensus* is assenting to the truth of that information.
   a. We have to believe that the information about Jesus—His person and His work—is a reality.
   b. Saving faith requires an intellectual, cognitive assent to the truth of the data.
   c. Demons even have *notitia* and *assensus* because they know the information and know it to be true.
3. *Fiducia* is placing trust in the information that is true.
   a. *Fiducia* requires trust along with intellectual awareness and assent.
      i. This is critical to the doctrine of justification by faith.
   b. Our trust and reliance on the work of Christ alone is the most important component to the profession of faith.
      i. A great problem is distinguishing faith from profession of faith.
      ii. Jesus Christ warned about false profession (Matt. 7:21–23; 15:8).
      iii. The danger of false profession is apparent in methods of decisional evangelism that attempt to manipulate people.
   c. *Notitia* and *assensus* are essential to *fiducia*.
      i. David Hume understood that people could make decisions to do things for all sorts of reasons, but people cannot make a decision to believe something they don't believe.
      ii. A person doesn't merely decide to believe in Jesus as Lord and Savior but is persuaded and enabled to trust Him.

C. What does the word *alone* mean in the formula of justification by faith alone?

1. The word *alone* means that there is no admixture of works in our faith as the basis for God's declaring us righteous.
2. A way to simplify the various views on justification is by creating a simple equation that resembles 2+2=4.
   a. The Roman Catholic formula is faith + works = justification.
   b. The antinomian formula is faith = justification – works.
      i. Antinomians believe that a person can be a true believer and never have any works.
   c. The Reformed formula is faith = justification + works.
      i. True faith will manifest itself by works of obedience after justification.
      ii. The works themselves contribute nothing to justification because justification has already taken place.
      iii. Luther's said it perfectly: "Justification is by faith alone but not by a faith that is alone."

3. Justification by faith alone is justification by Christ alone.
   a. We cannot add anything to or subtract anything from the merit of Christ.
   b. Christ saves us, so we can truly say, "We believe in justification by works," because they are His works.
   c. Christ fulfilled the law perfectly in His active obedience, and God transfers Christ's righteousness to us.
   d. Even though "by works of the law no human being will be justified" (Rom. 3:20a), we are nevertheless justified by faith in the One who did keep the works of the law.

D. Further distinctions can be made between the Roman Catholic and the Reformed views of justification and imputation.
1. The Roman Catholic view is analytical.
   a. An analytical statement adds nothing to the predicate that is not found in the subject because an analytical statement is true by definition.
      i. "A bachelor is an unmarried man" is an analytical statement, because a bachelor is by definition an unmarried man.
   b. The Roman Catholic view is analytical because God declares a person to be just only if that person is just.
2. The Reformed view is synthetic.
   a. A synthetic statement is a statement where there is something added in the information in the predicate that is not found in the subject.
      i. "The bachelor is a wealthy man" is a synthetic statement, because being a bachelor doesn't imply that one is wealthy.
   b. The Reformed view is synthetic because God adds Christ's righteousness to unjust sinners.
3. Both Protestants and Catholics use the term *forensic*.
   a. The term *forensic* is used because justification is a legal declaration by which God judicially declares us to be just.
   b. Forensic justification has been used as shorthand to describe the Protestant view of justification.
      i. Justification takes place when God declares a person is just in the Roman Catholic view, so Catholics can use the term *forensic* to describe justification as well.
      ii. God is the One who declares a person righteous in both cases.
      iii. The difference is whether someone has an *inherent* righteousness or an *alien* righteousness.
4. The group Evangelicals and Catholics Together believed they had reached a substantive agreement regarding justification.
   a. The truth is that Rome has always taught a forensic justification and the issue of imputation is at the heart of the matter.
      i. We are either justified by our righteousness or by someone else's righteousness.
   b. The word *alone* stresses a justification found only in Christ.

STUDY QUESTIONS

1. Saving faith consists of _________ distinct elements.
    a. Two
    b. Three
    c. Seven
    d. Eight

2. *Assensus* is affirming the intellectual data of saving faith.
    a. True
    b. False

3. The Reformed view of justification is _________.
    a. Analytic
    b. Forensic
    c. Synthetic
    d. Dialectic

4. "The bachelor is a wealthy man" is an analytical statement.
    a. True
    b. False

5. The term "forensic" in the phrase "forensic justification" is a(n) _________ term.
    a. Ecclesiastical
    b. Theological
    c. Historical
    d. Legal

6. _________ is the key issue that separates Protestants and Catholics.
    a. Faith
    b. Imputation
    c. Forensic justification
    d. All of the above

DISCUSSION QUESTIONS

1. What is a common accusation against those who believe that justification is by faith alone? How would you answer such an accusation?

2. Why is fiducia the most important element of saving faith?

3. What is a major concern with decisional evangelism?

4. How can Protestants faithfully declare that they are justified by works?

7

Paul's Letter to the Romans

INTRODUCTION

Paul gives his most exhaustive treatment of the doctrine of justification by faith in his letter to the Romans. In this lesson, Dr. Sproul takes us through the most important passages of Romans and expands on the theological concepts contained within the doctrine of justification.

LESSON OBJECTIVES

1. To look at the doctrine of justification by faith alone from Scripture
2. To expand the doctrine of justification to include propitiation and expiation as well as Christ's active and passive obedience

SCRIPTURE READING

. . . so that He might be just and the justifier of the one who has faith in Jesus.

—Romans 3:26b

LECTURE OUTLINE

A. The doctrine of justification by faith alone is extensively developed in Paul's letter to the Romans.
   1. The first section of Romans sets up the doctrine of justification by faith.
      a. Paul begins with the idea of the universal judgment of God upon a fallen humanity that suppresses knowledge of Him.
      b. Paul shows how the effects of sin have taken hold of all people, both Jew and Greek alike.
      c. Paul brings the entire world before the bar of God's justice.

2. Paul expounds on the nature of human sinfulness by quoting the Psalms.
   a. His quotations from the Psalms begin in Romans 3:11 and end in Romans 3:18.
3. Paul uses the metaphor of the "stopped mouth" before the judgment seat of God.
   a. It is a pure exercise in futility to give an excuse to God for our disobedience when His holiness, justice, and judgment are evident.

B. Romans 3:20 has been the subject of much debate in the history of theology and is important for our understanding of the doctrine of justification.
   1. Some believe that "by the deeds of the law" refers to the ceremonial requirements of the Old Testament law.
      a. No one will be justified by through the sacrificial system and cultic practices associated with the tabernacle and the temple.
      b. This is a very restrictive application of this text.
   2. The vast majority of commentators believe that "by deeds of the law" refers to all of the obligations of God's law including the moral obligations.
      a. Any good work is excluded from the grounds of justification.
   3. Others believe that "by deeds of the law" refers to works of obedience before regeneration.
      a. The Protestant and Roman views of justification are at odds with each other at this point as works are reintroduced for justification.
         i. Works may contribute to our reward in heaven, but they are never a part of our justification.

C. There is a difference between being pardoned and being justified.
   1. Justification is not simply divine pardon.
      a. Pardon is issued after a person is declared guilty, but the essence of justification is declaring a person just.
      b. Pardon is not necessary for someone who has been declared just.
   2. Justification goes beyond the forgiveness of sins.
      a. We are not only forgiven; we are declared righteous before God.
   3. The imputation of Christ's righteousness is fundamental to our understanding of justification.
      a. Romans 3:21–22 revisits the "righteousness of God" found in Romans 1:17 that is the righteousness that God gives to us.

D. We must make a distinction between Christ's passive and active obedience and between propitiation and expiation.
   1. Christ's passive obedience refers to His willingness to die for our sins in obedience to the Father.
      a. Paul refers to this as the "redemption that is in Christ Jesus" (Rom. 3:24).
   2. Propitiation and expiation are accomplished at Christ's death on the cross, and the cross is also a simple way to describe the difference between the two.
      a. The cross can be used to describe the difference between propitiation and expiation in that the cross has a vertical and horizontal beam.

   b. The vertical beam describes propitiation as a vertical transaction in which God's just demands are satisfied.
      i. That Christ was a perfect sacrifice is also an element of His active obedience.
   c. The horizontal beam describes expiation as a horizontal transaction in which Christ removes our sins as far as the east is from the west.
3. Propitiation and expiation are also modeled in the Old Testament sacrificial system on the Day of Atonement.
   a. The blood of one animal was poured on the mercy seat of the ark of the covenant as a covering and reconciliation to satisfy God's justice.
   b. The priest placed his hands on a second animal, the scapegoat, to symbolically transfer the sins of the people to it and drove it into the wilderness.
      i. The wilderness was understood to be outside the camp, outside of God's presence.
      ii. Christ suffers outside of the camp as the sins of the people are placed upon Him while He died the cursed death of the cross.
4. Christ's active obedience refers to His perfect life under the law.
   a. Christ is the new Adam, and He lived a life of perfect obedience, unlike the old Adam, who fell into disobedience and ruin.
   b. Christ had to live a life of perfect obedience so that His merit could be transferred to us.
      i. Christ did more than merely pay for our sins, because He lived a perfect life instead of simply coming to die in our place.
      ii. He fully submitted Himself to the law of God.
5. In our justification, Christ's righteousness is transferred to us, as our sin was transferred to Him on the cross.
   a. God demonstrated that Christ's sacrifice was satisfactory by raising Him for our justification (Rom. 4:25).
      i. His passive and active obedience satisfied the Father.
      ii. The Father raised Him to show that the work of redemption had indeed brought reconciliation.
6. Why did God have to go about saving us in this manner?
   a. God will never negotiate His righteousness and saves us in a manner by which He can retain His own righteousness.
   b. God maintains His justice by imputing our sins to Christ and His righteousness to us.

E. Paul proves his case for justification by faith apart from works of the law by the life of Abraham.
   1. Paul begins his examination of Abraham after concluding that one is "justified by faith apart from works of the law" (Rom. 3:28).
      a. There is no ground for boasting.
   2. Abraham believed the promises of God, and it was counted to him for righteousness (Gen. 15:6).

   a. Notice that God reckons Abraham as righteous the moment he puts his faith and trust in God.
3. Abraham is counted righteous before he is circumcised and before he offers Isaac on the altar.

F. Justification is indelibly linked to grace.
   1. *Sola fide* and *sola gratia* are inseparably related in the Reformed tradition, because the justification we receive is clearly by grace.
      a. God does not impute to us the sins we deserve, but rather imputes them to Jesus who covers us (Ps. 32:1–2).
   2. The motif of covering is found throughout the Bible.
      a. God makes clothes to cover the shame of Adam and Eve after the fall.
      b. Blood covers the mercy seat on the Day of Atonement.
      c. Christ covers our nakedness, our filthy rags, with His robe of righteousness.
   3. The only righteousness we need to stand before God was provided for us.

STUDY QUESTIONS

1. Rome takes the "works of the law" in Romans 3:20 to refer to _________ works of the law.
   a. All
   b. Moral
   c. Ceremonial
   d. Pre-regenerational

2. Justification is closely related to the idea of divine pardon.
   a. True
   b. False

3. God's removing our sins as far as the east is from the west is a picture of _________.
   a. Expiation
   b. Propitiation
   c. Justification
   d. Imputation

4. _________ involves the satisfaction of God's just demands.
   a. Expiation
   b. Propitiation
   c. Justification
   d. Imputation

5. Propitiation and expiation are both a part of Christ's active obedience.
   a. True
   b. False

6. Paul uses _________ to prove his case for justification by faith.
   a. Isaac
   b. David
   c. Rahab
   d. Abraham

DISCUSSION QUESTIONS

1. How can the cross be used as a metaphor to teach the difference between propitiation and expiation?

2. In what ways does the scapegoat prefigure Christ?

3. What is the significance of the resurrection in the doctrine of justification?

4. How would you answer someone who objects to the manner in which God decided to save us, claiming that there could have been a better way?

8

The Consequences of Justification

INTRODUCTION

Justification by faith gives us peace with, access to, and hope in a holy God. In this lesson, Dr. Sproul continues his study of justification in Paul's letter to the Romans by introducing the results of justification in the life of the believer.

LESSON OBJECTIVES

1. To survey the benefits that flow from justification
2. To properly order justification as preceding sanctification

SCRIPTURE READING

Since, therefore, we have now been justified by his blood, much more shall we be saved by Him from the wrath of God.

—Romans 5:9

LECTURE OUTLINE

A. What are the consequences of justification?
   1. Sometimes it is important to ask the simple question "So what?" when thinking about a theological issues.
      a. When considering the question "So what?" in relation to justification, we are concerned with the consequences or results of justification.
   2. After proving the doctrine of justification by faith alone in the life of Abraham, Paul begins the fifth chapter in his letter to the Romans with "Therefore."
      a. "Therefore" indicates a conclusion to an argument or a very significant point that depends on everything that came before it.

3. Paul follows "Therefore" with "having been justified by faith."
    a. This clearly shows that justification is a past event that has already occurred.
    b. The consequences of our justification follow this phrase.

B. The first consequence of our justification is that "we have peace with God through our Lord Jesus Christ" (Rom. 5:1).
1. One of the most important concepts related to the idea of peace with God is the idea of reconciliation.
    a. Estrangement is essential to understanding reconciliation, because people who are not estranged do not need reconciliation.
    b. The New Testament makes it clear that in our fallen condition we are at enmity with God and want nothing to do with Him.
    c. Those that deny God's existence in actuality know that He exists; they have a moral problem with Him and need to be reconciled to Him.
    d. The image conveyed in Scripture is that in our natural state we hate God and are at war with Him.
2. When God declares peace, we are reconciled to Him forever.
    a. When World War II ended, the announcement of peace was joyous and exhilarating occasion, but the peace enjoyed between nations doesn't ever last.
    b. When God makes a peace treaty, there can never again be the threat of war.
        i. Christians have the peace of the Prince of Peace but often neglect talking about its significance (John 14:27).
        ii. Luther said that the pagan trembles at the rustling of the leaf because in his reconciled state he fears the wrath of God.
        iii. Salvation is simultaneously by God and from God, so a Christian need not fear His wrath.

C. The second consequence of our justification is that "through him we have also obtained access by faith into this grace in which we stand" (Rom. 5:2).
1. When Adam and Eve were banished from the garden of Eden, God placed an angel with a flaming sword to prevent them from returning.
    a. Through Christ, that flaming sword has been removed.
    b. Likewise, the curtain of the temple has been torn.
2. We have the access of children who have been adopted into the family of God.
    a. We can now call God our "Father."
3. The Bible calls us to draw near to God and prepare ourselves for coming into the presences of God.
    a. God is everywhere and yet there are special manifestations of His presence.
    b. God specially manifests His presence in church.
        i. This should inform how we dress for worship, because we are coming into the presence of the Holy One from whom we were once banished and forbidden to enter.

        ii. We should come to church in a spirit of reverence and awe, a spirit of joy and comfort, for the peace we have with God.
    c. When we draw near to God, we draw near to God in Christ.
        i. Our Redeemer brings us into God's presence.
4. The Bible teaches us to "believe into" Christ.
    a. The Greek preposition *eis* can be understood as moving through a door from one room to another.
    b. We are likewise called to believe into Jesus for our justification.
5. Paul constantly uses the language of being "in Christ."
    a. We are in Christ, and Christ is in us.
    b. Everyone who is justified is brought from outside to inside.
    c. This should inform how Christians ought to love one another.
        i. How can you hate someone who is in Christ if you are also in Christ?
        ii. Christians have been brought into a family together.
    d. Paul's conversion teaches us the great unity there is between Christ and believers.
        i. As Paul was traveling on the road to Damascus, Jesus asked him, "Saul, Saul, why do you persecute me?" (Acts 9:4).
        ii. Paul, in persecuting believers, was persecuting Christ.
        iii. The union a believer has with Christ is also a union with other believers.

D. The third consequence of our justification is that "we rejoice in hope of the glory of God" (Rom. 5:2).
1. Hope is an outworking of faith and justification.
2. In the New Testament, hope is not a feeling associated with a desire or wish.
    a. Hope is the certainty of that which is to come in the future.
    b. Hope gives stability to believers that they will see the glory of God.
3. Paul goes on to say that "hope does not put us to shame" (Rom. 5:5).
    a. Our hope cannot fail because God keeps His promises.
4. The assurance of God's promises is the grounds of our sanctification.
    a. We do not work out our salvation with fear and trembling as if it were an uncertainty (Phil. 2:12–14).
    b. Assurance of salvation leads to conformity to Christ in our sanctification (2 Peter 2:10).
5. The relationship between justification and sanctification is critical to resolving Paul's teaching of justification with the teaching of James' epistle.

STUDY QUESTIONS

1. __________ is not a consequence of our justification.
    a. Peace
    b. Access
    c. Hope
    d. Faith

2. A concept that is essential to understanding reconciliation is ________.
    a. Estrangement
    b. Rebellion
    c. Warfare
    d. Exile

3. People who question the existence of God most likely have an intellectual problem with God.
    a. True
    b. False

4. Christians often do not adequately highlight the importance of ________ as a consequence of justification.
    a. Peace
    b. Faith
    c. Hope
    d. Love

5. Believers are ultimately saved from ________.
    a. Sin
    b. Hell
    c. Death
    d. God

6. A major part of the access that we have with God in our justification is ________.
    a. Sanctification
    b. Adoption
    c. Peace
    d. Hope

DISCUSSION QUESTIONS

1. Why are the concepts of reconciliation and estrangement important for the defense of the Christian faith to unbelievers?

2. What is the significance of God being the one who declared peace with us?

3. How should "access to God" inform our worship?

4. How does understanding justification change the way we relate to other Christians?

9

Paul vs. James?

INTRODUCTION

Paul's epistle to the Romans is not irreconcilable with the epistle of James. In this lesson, Dr. Sproul explains how we are to understand two seemingly contradictory portions of Scripture that deal with the doctrine of justification.

LESSON OBJECTIVES

1. To resolve Paul's teaching on justification with the epistle of James
2. To expand on the nature of regeneration and faith

SCRIPTURE READING

Of His own will He brought us forth by the word of truth.

—James 1:18a

LECTURE OUTLINE

A. How do we reconcile what Paul teaches in Romans with the epistle of James?
   1. Roman Catholics used the second chapter of James to refute to the assertion that justification is by faith alone: "You see a person is justified by works and not by faith alone" (James 2:24).
      a. This is an explicit statement from Scripture that would seem to be a crushing blow to the doctrine of justification by faith alone.
   2. Many people believe that what Paul teaches in Romans is irreconcilable to the epistle of James.
      a. In order to understand how such a seeming contradiction could arise, some have believed that it is important to know which was written first.
      b. Some argue that Paul is refuting James while others argue that James is refuting Paul.

   c. Classic orthodoxy would say that neither Paul nor James was trying to refute one another and that the two positions are not contradictory.

B. Part of the difficulty is that Paul and James use the same word for justification and the same person to build their case.
   1. Paul and James both use the word *dikaiosunē* for justification, and they both use Abraham to prove their point.
      a. Paul references Abraham's justification as found in Genesis 15 while James references Abraham's justification as found in Genesis 22.
   2. The difficulty in reconciling Paul and James caused Luther to once question the canonicity of James.
      a. Luther repented of his judgment of James as an "epistle of straw."
      b. Scholars have attempted to twist Luther's questioning the canonicity of James to prove that he did not believe in the inerrancy of Scripture.
      c. Luther was simply questioning whether Scripture contained the book of James, not the inerrancy of Scripture.

C. *Dikaiosunē* can have more than one meaning.
   1. Christ uses the word *dikaiosunē* when stating, "Wisdom is justified by her children" (Luke 7:35).
   a. This obviously does not mean that wisdom is reconciled to God by having babies but that wisdom is shown to be wisdom by its fruit.
      i. As an aside, many New Testament scholars consider the book of James as part of the wisdom literature of the Bible.
      ii. It follows much of the same literary forms found in the Old Testament Wisdom Literature.
   b. Christ's use of the word "justified" means to demonstrate or manifest the truth of something.

D. It is important to ask the question, "What problem is James trying to solve?"
   1. James is dealing with the question of people who make a profession of faith but do not manifest any fruit (James 2:14).
      a. Paul, on the other hand, is dealing with the question of how an unjust person can stand in the presence of a just and holy God.
      b. Paul is ultimately concerned with a person's justification before God while James is concerned with a person's profession of faith.
   2. James is concerned with making a distinction between a dead faith and a living faith (James 2:17).
      a. Luther was confronted with the claim that the doctrine of justification by faith alone allows people to live in whatever way they please.
      b. Luther believed that the faith that justifies is a *fides viva*, a living faith, which manifests itself in the fruit of obedience.
      c. Paul was also confronted with this line of questioning and responded with a resounding "God forbid!" (Rom. 6:2a).

3. James is looking at justification from a different perspective.
    a. The only way to evaluate the truth of another person's profession of faith is by how it manifests itself in a person's life (Matt. 7:20).
    b. God knows the heart and knows when a profession of faith is genuine.

E. James and Paul appealed to Abraham at different times in his life.
1. Paul proves that justification is by faith by pointing to Genesis 15 where Abraham is counted as righteous for believing God's promise.
2. James proves Abraham's justification by works by pointing to Genesis 22 where Abraham is ready to sacrifice Isaac on the altar.
    a. James is not referring to Abraham's justification before God but the evidence of Abraham's faith before men.
    b. The only kind of faith that saves is a living faith made manifest by works, so Abraham is demonstrating his claim of faith.
    c. This is contrary to antinomianism and the idea of a carnal Christian.
3. James is speaking about Abraham's being vindicated by his profession of faith with the works that flow from it.
a. There is no contradiction between Paul and James.

F. The *ordo salutis*—order of salvation—is important to round out our discussion of justification by faith alone.
1. The phrase *regeneration precedes faith* captures the essence of Reformed theology and answers the question, "Where does saving faith come from?"
    a. Faith is not an act of our will working independently of God.
    b. God sovereignly changes the disposition of our hearts and gives us saving faith by the immediate, supernatural work of the Holy Spirit.
2. The *ordo salutis* concerns the logical order of salvation.
    a. The *ordo salutis* does not describe the temporal order of salvation.
    b. Justification is simultaneous with saving faith, but faith precedes justification in terms of its logical order.
3. The majority of evangelical Christians believe that faith precedes regeneration.
    a. They believe that rebirth is a result of believing in Christ.
    b. Rather, a person must be born again and spiritually made alive to have faith (John 3:1–8; Eph. 2:5).
    c. God the Holy Spirit changes the disposition of the heart so that the person who refused to believe can embrace the truth in faith.
4. Jonathan Edwards' sermon "A Divine and Supernatural Light" is about the work of the Holy Spirit in regeneration.
    a. The Holy Spirit works in such a way that we not only see the truth of a proposition but also the loveliness of it, so that the Holy Spirit creates the faith that justifies us.
    b. We are taken from a state of spiritual death to spiritual life, and the rest of the Christian life is marked by the war between flesh and Spirit.

5. Paul's abbreviated list of the order of salvation in Romans 8 helps to further our understanding of regeneration.
    a. Those whom God foreknew He also predestined, called, justified, and glorified (Rom. 8:29–30).
    b. Paul is referring to the inward call of Holy Spirit as opposed to the outward call of the gospel.
    c. It is the effectual inward call of God by which we are brought to a faith that is a living faith through which we are justified.

STUDY QUESTIONS

1. It is important to know which book was written first in order to reconcile Romans with James.
    a. True
    b. False
2. Paul and James both use Abraham and _________ in their arguments.
    a. Isaac
    b. Rahab
    c. *Dikaiosunē*
    d. *Iustificare*
3. Luther once questioned the _________ of James.
    a. Authenticity
    b. Canonicity
    c. Accuracy
    d. All of the above
4. Jonathan Edwards' "A Divine and Supernatural Light" is about the Holy Spirit and _________.
    a. Justification
    b. Sanctification
    c. Regeneration
    d. Glorification
5. The *ordo salutis* refers to the temporal order of salvation.
    a. True
    b. False
6. _________ answered the challenges to justification by faith by stressing the faith had to be a *fides vive*.
    a. Paul
    b. Calvin
    c. Luther
    d. Edwards

DISCUSSION QUESTIONS

1. What evidence from Martin Luther's life do we have to understand the complexity of harmonizing Paul with James?

2. What did Dr. Sproul suggest as a strategy for understanding the epistle of James in relation to Paul's teaching on justification?

3. How does the appeal to Abraham differ from Paul to James?

4. How can you use the epistle of James to combat antinomianism?

10

Questions and Answers

INTRODUCTION

We have now examined the doctrine of justification historically, theologically, and scripturally. In this final lesson, Dr. Sproul concludes our study by answering questions that help underline the fact that justification is indeed by faith alone.

LESSON OBJECTIVE

To answer questions raised concerning the doctrine of justification

SCRIPTURE READING

For if, because of one man's trespass, death reigned through that one man, much more will those who receive the abundance of grace and the free gift of righteousness reign in life through the one man Jesus Christ.

—Romans 5:17

LECTURE OUTLINE

A. How can a Christian know that he is saved?
   1. The question of assurance is not an abstract theological curiosity.
      a. The question is deeply personal, as it has to do with our status before God.
      b. Peter stressed the importance of assurance for our sanctification (2 Peter 1:10).
   2. The practical approach to dealing with someone who is questioning their salvation is to ask a series of questions.
      a. Do you love Christ *perfectly*?
      b. Do you love Christ *as much as you should* love Him?
      c. Do you love Christ as presented in the New Testament *at all*?
      d. How can you possibly have any affection for Jesus unless you are born of the Holy Spirit?

3. The theological approach to dealing with someone who is questioning their salvation follows naturally from the questions above.
    a. The proper conclusion from the questions above will help a person understand that they could not love Christ apart from the new birth.
    b. If they are partakers of the new birth, it is by God's sovereign choice to regenerate them.
    c. God will complete the work He began, and thus a person can have full assurance of his salvation.

B. Does God cooperate with us in our sanctification?
1. The classic text to answer that question is "work out your own salvation with fear and trembling, for it is God who works in you, both to will and to work for His good pleasure" (Phil. 2:12–13)
2. Regeneration is the sovereign, monergistic work of God the Holy Spirit.
    a. Monergism means "one working."
    b. God is the only one who is active in regeneration.
3. The rest of the process of salvation is a synergistic, cooperative work.
    a. We are not passive in our sanctification.
    b. Our sanctification is to be a diligent labor that we undertake knowing that we have the grace of God working in us.

C. How important is the teaching of the passive and active obedience of Christ?
1. J. Gresham Machen's last words in a telegram to his colleagues at Westminster Theological Seminary in Philadelphia were: "Grateful for the active obedience of Christ. No hope without it."
    a. Machen died of pneumonia when, despite a severe cold, he took a speaking engagement in North Dakota during the middle of winter.
    b. Machen understood the importance of the active and passive obedience of Christ.
2. In the attempts to bridge the divide over the doctrine of justification, there has been a renewed attack against the active obedience of Christ particularly.
    a. The single concept that could not be resolved during the sixteenth century, continuing to this day, was imputation.
    b. Without the imputed, active obedience of Christ, there are no grounds for justification, and that means there is no gospel.
3. Dispensationalists reject the distinction between the covenant of works and the covenant of grace.
    a. Rejecting this distinction causes them to reject the active obedience of Christ.
4. In Reformed thought, the covenant of works is the original covenant that God made with Adam and Eve.
    a. God still provides a way for salvation and promises to crush the serpent, so every relationship with God after the fall is gracious.

        i. It is argued that God was not obliged to covenant with us in the first place, so the distinction between the covenant of works and the covenant of grace is not necessary.
        ii. This argument does not acknowledge that the distinction is made because of Christ's work as the new Adam.
    b. Jesus takes upon Himself the responsibility to fulfill the original covenant as the new Adam in His active obedience.
        i. Adam's disobedience brought death; Christ's obedience brought life (Rom. 5:12–21).
    c. The denial of Christ's active obedience attacks the distinction between the covenant of grace and the covenant of works.
    d. Without Christ's active obedience, there is no redemption.

D. Why is it hard to recognize the depth of our own sin?
1. One of the consequences of original sin is that we are blinded to the full reality of the sinfulness of sin.
    a. Coming to a deeper understanding of the sinfulness of sin is a mark of sanctification and growth in grace.
2. We have a tendency to protect ourselves from the full realization of our sinfulness by judging ourselves by our own standard and by those around us.
    a. Nathan's parable of the rich man exposed David to his sin and led him to pen the model prayer of confession and contrition, Psalm 51.
3. God does not discipline us by instantaneously revealing the true depths of our sin out of His kindness, because we wouldn't be able to handle it.
    a. Satan accuses you of the same sin of which the Spirit convicts you.
    b. Satan's purpose is to destroy you, but the Spirit aims to redeem you.
4. The only way to understand the degree of our sin is by studying the character of God.
    a. When Isaiah stood before God, he saw who God was, understood himself before a holy God, and pronounced upon himself a curse.
5. A large majority of evangelical and Roman Catholics responded to a recent survey that they do not believe the smallest sin to be cosmic treason.
    a. Even the smallest sin is cosmic treason, though not all sins are equally heinous.
    b. People who think otherwise have not come to grips with the character of God as the standard for their own character.

E. What are the challenges to the doctrine of justification today?
1. There is the challenge of those who do not believe they need to be justified.
2. There is the challenge that the doctrine of justification is not as important as the Reformers thought it to be.
    a. Even though people are no longer killing each other over the issue of justification, it is still at the very heart of the gospel.

3. There are attempts to reconcile Protestants and Catholics at the expense of the doctrine of justification.
    a. The Lutheran church has reached some agreement with Rome over justification.
    b. The Evangelical and Catholics Together (ECT) initiative claimed to have reached a unity of faith in the gospel.
        i. Catholics who affirm the Council of Trent signed the initiative.
    c. The ECT released a second version of the statement but no resolution has been made on imputation.
4. There have been recent controversies over the doctrine of justification.
    a. A professor from Westminster Theological Seminary was removed from his position in the 1980s because he began to believe works were a necessary part of justification.
    b. N.T. Wright is a popular theologian who believes that justification is more of a matter of covenant status in Second Temple Judaism.
5. There is still the ongoing debate about the lordship of Christ.
    a. Some believe Jesus can be their Savior and not receive Him as Lord.

F. How did Martin Luther's pastoral crises affect his theology, and how did they affect his work?
1. Luther believed every generation has to fight for the gospel, because if the gospel is preached clearly and boldly, it will create conflict.
2. Luther's concern in writing the Ninety-Five Theses was to guard against the potential corrupting influence to God's people from the sale of indulgences.
3. Luther's courage in the recovery of the gospel should be rightly praised, yet he never developed a strong Christology in line with Chalcedon.

STUDY QUESTIONS

1. Peter stresses that we make our calling and election sure for the sake of our __________.
    a. Justification
    b. Regeneration
    c. Sanctification
    d. All of the above

2. Synergism means "one working."
    a. True
    b. False

3. The active obedience of Christ is primary to _________.
   a. Imputation
   b. Regeneration
   c. Sanctification
   d. Propitiation

4. According to Dr. Sproul, the smallest sin is an act of _________ treason.
   a. Galactic
   b. Cosmic
   c. Universal
   d. Celestial

5. An appropriate way to deepen our understanding of our own sinfulness is to look at the sins of others.
   a. True
   b. False

6. The model prayer of confession and contrition is found in _________.
   a. Psalm 119
   b. Psalm 51
   c. Psalm 23
   d. Psalm 19

DISCUSSION QUESTIONS

1. How can you help someone who is struggling with assurance of salvation?

2. Why is the active obedience of Christ so critical in the discussion of justification?

3. What is one important mark in your sanctification and growth in grace?

4. How does Satan's dealing with our sin differ from that of the Holy Spirit?

ANSWER KEY FOR STUDY QUESTIONS

Lesson 1
1. B
2. D
3. B
4. B
5. A

Lesson 2
1. B
2. C
3. C
4. B
5. B
6. B

Lesson 3
1. B
2. B
3. C
4. D
5. B
6. D

Lesson 4
1. B
2. B
3. C
4. D
5. A
6. B

Lesson 5
1. B
2. B
3. C
4. B
5. B
6. D

Lesson 6
1. B
2. B
3. C
4. B
5. D
6. B

Lesson 7
1. D
2. B
3. A
4. B
5. A
6. D

Lesson 8
1. D
2. A
3. B
4. A
5. D
6. B

Lesson 9
1. B
2. C
3. B
4. C
5. B
6. C

Lesson 10
1. C
2. B
3. A
4. B
5. B
6. B